SURVIVE

LIVE

or

THRIVE

Simple Life Tips for Those Who Feel Stuck in a Rut

by

L. LYNN GILLIARD

Survive, Live or Thrive?
Published by: Venup Publishing
LifeLoveLynn.com

ISBN 978-0-9836392-4-4

Table of Contents

Introduction

I get so many inspirations during the course of a day—stuff that I want to share as soon as the thought comes to me, but the ideas flow so quickly that I often feel a bit overwhelmed with them. I'm not sure what to focus on or where to begin. So I decided to write this book as a start, to get some of these thoughts, inspirations and learning experiences out into the world.

Let's get right down to business. This book is meant to get you thinking about your life and what's important. It continually asks the question: **"are you surviving, living or thriving in the various important areas of your life?"**

What is surviving? Barely making it. Keeping your head over water.

What is living? Existing. Everything is copasetic and fairly normal, but you're not all the way happy and fulfilled.

What is thriving? It is feeling excited about your life. It's waking up early in the morning eager and ready to start your day. It's having the ultimate relationships that nourish your soul. It's having a zest for life that's indescribable.

The goal of this book is to help you (and me) get closer and closer to thriving in every area of our lives.

The areas that I address in this book include:

- pursuing your dreams
- making good money
- dating and love relationships
- family and other relationships
- self-love (loving yourself)

While this book specifically speaks to women in some places, the lessons actually apply to everyone. It applies to people from all walks of life, of all backgrounds and of all sexual orientations.

In this book I discuss how we are mostly unaware of our potential to do wonderful things and live a beautiful life due to fear, low self-esteem and the wool that has been pulled over our eyes thanks to all of the negative messages that swirl around us every day. I also discuss the idea that if we're not where we want to be in our lives (thriving) we can't blame anyone but ourselves for that.

Here's a post that I wrote about how we sometimes allow the world to put us in the "dunce corner" of life, where we feel stupid, useless and inferior:

Blog Post—1/26/14—Life Love Lynn

Have You Allowed the World to Put You in "Your Place?"

Are you deliriously happy? If you are, congratulations—you are doing life right. We're not meant to be struggling through life—we're supposed to be living it up.

But if you cannot honestly say that you are deliriously happy with the way your life is going, keep reading.

There's a good chance that you are where you are right now in life because you have allowed the opinions, thoughts, actions and words of other people to pigeonhole you into a certain station in life.

We create and form our reality. What we accept for ourselves is what we get.

Someone, maybe a parent, sibling or peer, insulted you throughout your younger years. Eventually you started to believe that characterization of who you are.

A mean, miserable teacher told you that the only job you would be good at is working at a grocery store. So instead of pursuing a job or career in the field of your choice you continue to work in retail stores. (In fact, schools often shape our futures by forcing us to choose a major without giving us proper counseling about this major life decision.)

Your friends taught you that drinking and getting drop down drunk every weekend or taking drugs is normal, so that's what you continue to do week after week.

You were told since a young child that getting married and having babies is crucial to being a happy normal woman. But here's a newsflash: a lot of married women with kids are absolutely miserable! Some young women may be happier if they follow a different path early on before settling down.

Someone may have told you that your skin color wasn't the "right" shade, or that you weren't attractive enough, or that you're not the right size, so you believed those things and took a certain path in life based on that information.

Words can be powerful. Accepting a negative affirmation into your reality is almost like taking a spoonful of slow acting poison that breaks down your life force little by little every day. Accepting the opinions and beliefs of others into your reality can cause low self-esteem, which causes you to live a less fulfilling life. Low self-esteem prevents you from dreaming big.

How can we ever manage to live a life that makes us happy if we're living our lives based on what other people want or see for us?

What do YOU really want for your life? What do YOU see for yourself? Where do YOU want to be? Who do YOU want to share your life with?

If you're not happy with the way your life has been going, start answering these questions.

Then start envisioning the answers manifesting in your life.

Then start living your life the way it was meant to be lived!

Love Lynn

Part I: Pursuing Your Dreams

"You're either creating, or you are disintegrating."

-- Les Brown

When it comes to pursuing your dreams, are you **surviving, living or thriving**?

I believe that one definition of happiness is feeling that you are progressing forward toward something in your life.

When you feel like you're not going anywhere in your life, you feel miserable, stagnant and angry at everyone and everything.

But when you're working toward your dreams and goals, it feels ohhh soooo good. You wake up ridiculously early in the morning and get right to work. You feel as if birds are tweeting beautiful songs around your head as you create and innovate.

I have lived both of these experiences. When I came out of school, I found myself stuck in a dead end job in the corporate world. I was so unbelievably unhappy with my job because I knew that 10 years later I'd probably be in the same exact place at the company (or possibly even lower on the totem pole).

Then I set forth on a new journey shortly after starting that job to start my own business and the feeling of elation, due to the belief that I was now going somewhere, was overwhelmingly wonderful.

"Life happened" since that time, as it usually does, and I lost my motivation after a number of setbacks.

Only recently did that excitement return when I got the inspiration to write my dating guide for women entitled *Let Him Chase You*. When the message came to me, I literally jumped out of my seat and started writing immediately. For months before that, I don't think I wrote one word due to depression over a sad experience in my life.

I still get those spurts of energy and excitement when I'm working on a new project, like this book that you're reading now. When I really get started, I'm unstoppable. I love to make my ideas real.

People from all walks of life go through these ups and downs.

For instance, some women with children find themselves unhappy and unfulfilled. They feel as if they've pigeon-holed themselves into a place where they can't escape—a place where they can't progress forward in life.

And it's not just women of course—some men go through this as well. They find themselves working the same boring, mechanical job day in and out that isn't going to take them anywhere but closer and closer to retirement. They want more but they don't know how to get it. They're not happy in their relationships and don't get along with many people. That is why a lot of people fill up the bars at 5 o'clock every day to drink away the pain.

In both cases, they're not progressing toward anything meaningful, and that makes them miserable.

But with just a slight change in mindset anyone can get started doing something special that they really love and the world will seem new and limitless again.

Limiting Beliefs

What stops us from going after our dreams? One answer is this: limiting beliefs.

My definition of a limiting belief is this: a recorder that's playing over and over in our heads of a negative message that was programmed into our thoughts many years before.

Examples of limiting beliefs:

- I'm not smart enough to speak in front of people

- I didn't go to an Ivy league school, so nobody cares what I have to say

- I'm always going to be broke

- I can't afford to start a business

- I'm too short to command respect from my peers

- I'm not pretty enough to deserve a good relationship

The list goes on and on. I believe it takes many years for a limiting belief to be firmly implanted in a person's mind to the point where she believes it to be the truth about her life. And in some cases, all it takes it one memorable negative experience to convince you that you can't.

For example, I've always known that I can hold a tune. But one day when I sang in front of a group of people who I considered to be my friends, one of them laughed and basically told me to leave the singing for Diana Ross. So what did I do? I laughed along with them and just stopped singing in public.

I allowed that limiting belief to stop me from doing something that I know, deep down, I'm good at. Who knows what blessings I could have brought to the world years ago with my voice if I hadn't allowed that limiting belief to plant itself in my life?

The truth is that our limiting beliefs hold us back from achieving true greatness in life. I don't fully understand it yet, but it seems as if the things that we don't believe are possible for our lives are the very things that we would thrive at if we only put some time and attention into them.

Fear of Failure and Fear of Success

Another reason why many of us do not go after our dreams wholeheartedly is FEAR: **False Evidence Appearing Real.**

There are two types of fears—the fear of failure and the fear of success. Both of them can prevent us from taking bold steps forward.

On one end we're afraid of falling flat on our faces if we take a chance, step out and do something different. That fear may be of going broke, being laughed at by our friends or of being judged by our family members.

Then there's a fear of success. Yes, some of us are afraid of what will happen if we actually become successful beyond anything we dreamed about. We may fear that it will estrange us from our family and friends, make people jealous or monopolize our lives in some way.

Fear is an illusion. Think about everything you're fearful of—where did that come from? It doesn't usually come from experiencing something firsthand, but from *hearing* something that someone told you or from seeing something on television. Those fears often hold us back from trying someone new and different in life. Even when something does happen to us firsthand, we take that as a cue to run and hide from taking more risks instead of using it as a learning experience to become even stronger than we were before.

Here's a redacted snippet from a blog post that I wrote about conquering our fears:

> **Blog Post—8/4/13—FWB Sucks**
>
> **Conquering Your Fears in Life**
>
> I recently faced one of my biggest fears head on—deep water.
>
> Though I can swim and have been able to swim for years now, I've still had a fear of wading on the deep side of the pool where I couldn't feel the floor with my feet.

This stems from a childhood experience where I almost drowned. I spent at least 5 minutes flailing, drinking water and wondering why I couldn't feel the ground under my feet. Someone had to save me. I was afraid of water for a long time after that.

Well, I finally decided that this would be the moment when I finally ventured to the 7 foot end of the pool. I had a couple of issues, but all in all it turned out to not be as scary as I thought it would be. I now swim like a fish.

Identify and face your … fear head on. Regardless of the result, smile and be thankful because YOU DID IT. And chances are it won't be as bad as you thought.

Love Lynn

The Will to Fail

Fear is a major enemy to our pursuit of success in life, but the real reason behind why we don't go after our dreams can get even more complicated than that. Early 20th century writer and author Dorothea Brande wrote about why we fail in her book Wake Up and Live! She discusses how some of us are actually committed to the "pursuit of failure" or the "will to fail." She says that there's a force within that actually inspires us to want to fail and give up in our lives. It inspires us to do things that will impede our progress, like wasting time, procrastinating, gambling, shopping too much, drinking too much, making excuses, watching mindless television shows or even eating bad foods and gaining weight. So maybe some of us don't pursue our dreams because that "urge" to fail within is too strong.

Figuring Out What You Want to Do With Your Life

Some people stay stuck in the same rut year in and year out simply because they don't know what they want to do yet. The inspiration isn't there yet.

Sometimes you have to actively seek out the answer. Get the ball rolling—set aside at least 30 minutes every day to write down all of the things that you LOVE to do and the things that you do well. This is a quick and simple way to get the brainstorming process started. You may find yourself struggling to write things down one day and on other days the ideas are flowing. Just be consistent.

Also, buy yourself a little hard cover journal or memo book to carry about with you everywhere you go. Write in it whenever you get an inspiration or idea.

Next, sit down and meditate or pray for a while. Ask God / Divine Providence / The Universe / The Power of All That's Good to open your mind to the right solution for your life.

Then, just listen and pay attention as opportunities, ideas and inspirations start to come into your life. For instance, if you decide that you want to earn money playing the piano, you might suddenly meet someone at a party who's looking for a piano teacher. If you want to become an event coordinator, maybe your friend or family member needs help organizing a special graduation party.

Finally, act. Don't sit on your hands when the inspiration or idea finally comes to you. You have to take action if you want to make things happen. Things don't have to be perfect before you begin; you'll learn, grow and tweak your plan as you go along. Just get started.

One Day, One Step at a Time

Many people don't take action to pursue their dreams because they are waiting for something to happen first. They're waiting for a big check to float out of the sky or for someone who wants to help them to knock on their door.

Maybe they're waiting until they're happy or until they're married or until they earn their MBA.

But these are all just excuses to postpone taking action NOW.

The sky doesn't have to open and heavenly music doesn't have to play for you to get started on your dreams. You can start TODAY.

How? The same way you manage to get from point A to point B every day. You put one foot in front of the other and start moving in one direction. You take one step at a time.

For instance, say your goal is to become a famous artist but you've never painted in your life. What can you do today to start on the path to that goal?

Get in your car and drive to the art store to buy some art supplies! Set up an easel in your backyard, garage or living room and have fun creating whatever the heck you want to create.

What about if you want to open up a franchise location for a popular business but you don't have any money?

You walk into the headquarters and ask for a brochure about franchising or you go to the business' website and request more information. You go to a franchising seminar or sign up for counseling at a Small Business Development Center. Who cares that you don't have the finances right now—life has a way of opening up opportunities to people who take action.

But you have to be serious about your dream. You can't half-ass it. You have to be consistent with your idea if you want it to become a reality. It might take months or even years for it to come to full fruition, but with consistency, openness, a plan of action and knowledge of your field it will happen for you.

It's Hard to Pursue Your Dreams When Your Attitude Stinks

It's so important to have a positive attitude and mindset each day if you want to successfully pursue your dreams. Your attitude determines everything from how your day will go to how people will relate to you. You don't have to take my word for it, just do this simple experiment:

> Wake up early in the morning tomorrow, stretch and say "this is going to be the best day ever!" It doesn't matter if you fully believe it just yet, just say it and say

> it like you mean it. Smile as you brush your teeth. Make a firm resolution that it doesn't matter what anyone says or does to you, how anyone looks at you or what you read or see on the television, you are going to smile your way through it and keep moving. Be aware of this resolution as you go through your day. Take note of how things go, the small blessings that come your way and how people relate with you.

If you commit yourself to this simple experiment, you'll find that something strange happens. You feel better about yourself and as a result, the people around you treat you better. The day seems to go easier. The grocery clerk smiles at you. Parking spaces open up right when you turn into the lot. You catch your trains right on time. Lunch tastes fresher and more delicious. And it all gets better and better each day.

When you live each day like this, doors and windows open up that makes it so much easier to turn your dreams into reality. You feel the urge to write or create. Ideas and resources flow to you. Good people come around you and encourage you. So it's crucial that you get your attitude in check if you want things to start going your way.

Women In Particular Often Shrink Due to Fear of What People Will Think

I specialize in writing about women's issues for obvious reasons, as I am a woman, but it's also because I see firsthand how women and girls limit themselves due to the messages that they receive from society. Women have amazing potential and talents but don't always boldly go after their dreams because of fear of what other people will think. We sometimes don't demand what we're worth or allow people to take our resources (the most precious of them being time) without requesting fair compensation in return.

I was listening to an audio book once where various people were telling their stories. The author graciously allowed each person to include his or her information at the end of each story, I assume in exchange for their submissions.

At the end, the women rushed through telling their names and website addresses. I could barely remember their names let alone their websites.

Then one man told his story and it was twice, maybe three times as long as the others. At the end, he said his website name not once, not twice, but three times and was sure to spell it out clearly.

I believe one of the reasons why men still out earn women (at least as of the date of this publishing) is that men aren't afraid to do what's necessary to ensure that they get the maximum exposure and profit for themselves and for their businesses. A lot of us women are more concerned about what people might think of us if we advocate for ourselves.

No matter your gender, you are deserving of the fullness and richness of life. If we allow ourselves to stay cornered by small and limiting thoughts, they will lead us to a small and limiting life.

To conclude this part of the book, here are three final tips that I've used personally to get motivated to pursue my dreams:

1. Write Things Down

Thoughts are fleeting. We have hundreds, maybe even thousands of them every day. I have learned to take the advice of countless wise people, like Napoleon Hill, and started writing things down in a journal (as mentioned earlier). I purchased a few small notebooks that I use to write down my ideas and inspirations. I also use my smartphone to write down notes but that isn't always as convenient.

I write down notes while I'm traveling, while I'm out having fun with friends and even when I've just woken up from a great dream. If I don't write down what I have on my mind within the hour, there's a good chance that it will leave me.

We are bombarded with so many different messages in the course of a day. This makes it extremely difficult to hold onto just one for any extended period of time. So keep a journal handy to write down everything that you think about that you believe is important.

2. Turn off the Television Man!

I am a freelancer, so I set my own schedule. I did a little mini experiment with myself one day. I measured how much work I completed while watching TV compared to how much work I completed while listening to a motivational tape.

The results, of course, showed that watching television was a major drain on my productivity. Listening to a motivational tape reduced the time it took to complete my task (writing for a client) by two or more hours. What I realized is that I could complete my task and then dedicate those extra two hours to leisurely watching the television program if I wanted. OR I could dedicate those extra two hours to more projects.

Do this experiment. Start a task while watching television, and then do the same exact task while listening to a motivational audiobook. You'll most likely find that listening to the audio book makes a lot more sense in your day.

3. Get Your OWN Personal Education

A lot of us are perfectly willing to spend thousands of dollars on a college education, but hesitant to spend $15 on a book that might teach us everything that we need to know on the subject! In fact, there is evidence that reading a certain number of books or listening to audiobooks can give you the equivalent of a college education after a period of time.

If you want to thrive in your pursuit of your dreams, you have to get serious about educating yourself regularly. The stuff you learned in school isn't enough.

There are countless books, audio books, guides and programs available that touch on every subject that you can imagine. There's also a wealth of free information available from doing Google keyword searches. And when you do Google something, don't just click the first link—explore the third, fourth, fifth page and beyond to learn new things.

Once you have a firm grasp of what you want to do, commit to reading at least one new book per week. Read your book on your lunch break at work and for at least an hour when you get home (the television can wait). Read your book on the train or while you're carpooling to work. Read your book when you're in a waiting room. Make it a habit.

If you drive to work and sit in traffic for an extended period of time, I can't stress the value of audiobooks enough. Audiobooks are what helped me get my life on the right track. Listen in your car, while cooking, while working out or anywhere you find yourself doing a monotonous activity that allows you to listen in. I really like to listen to audio books when I'm working or doing chores because it makes it go by quicker.

Part 9: Money—Are You Attracting or Repelling It

Carrying over from that previous conversation about pursuing our dreams, why is it that we are afraid of having success and the financial wealth that comes with it?

As I mentioned, one guess is that it's our inner fears tamping down our potential, because deep down, we are afraid of having success. We are afraid that if we achieve great success, it will create a whole new set of problems in our lives. We believe the saying "more money, more problems" when in actuality, the people who say that are just prone to problems. They love drama, like to flaunt their wealth and/or just don't know how to deal with other people effectively. There are some people who get blessed with a $10 bill and turn into instant assholes—you know the type!

Another guess is that we're allowing certain messages and ideas that have been programmed into our minds about ourselves prevent us from accept the possibility of being wealthy. Maybe we believe that we belong in a certain station in life and shouldn't dare try to do anything else. For instance, someone might be mentally saying "my grandpa worked at a factory all his life, my dad worked at a factory and so I'm going to work at a factory."

There's no question that money is a top concern on our minds. It may actually be THE top concern on some of our minds.

Money may not be everything, but it sure is something isn't it? Having money can make your life so much easier in so many ways.

So why is it that many of us still have such a negative mindset when it comes to money? Because some of us have been taught since we were kids that money is bad and people who have it are bad. We're taught that rich men can't make it into heaven and that being poor is admirable. That doesn't make sense

As you carry that mindset into your adulthood, is it any wonder that you don't have any money?

The truth is that God, The Universe or whatever you wish to call the force holding this earth on its axis wants us to be GREAT. And it order to be great, you need RESOURCES. And in order to have resources, you need to have MONEY.

So as far as your financial life, are you surviving, living or thriving?

Pick Up That Dime

One thing I've learned from my study of the law of attraction and other laws that govern the universe is that we have to be careful about the messages we're sending in even our smallest actions and words.

For instance, when you say "I'm broke," you just made a specific declaration to the world about your life. Instead of saying "I'm broke" say "I choose to use my resources in a different way" instead. That's a declaration that says you're still flush with cash but you want to use it for other things. Simple.

Another lesson I had to learn was that demonstrations matter when it comes to money flowing into your life. One day, I was boarding a bus and saw a shiny dime on the ground, gleaming up at me in the light. I looked at it and passed by it to give the clerk my ticket. When I sat down on the bus, a very strong voice said to me "GO PICK UP THAT DIME!"

I looked around at all of the people on the bus and thought about how they would probably judge me for getting back off of the bus just to pick a small coin up off of the concrete. I fought with myself for a while, but finally said to myself "why does the opinion of these people matter to me so much? I will probably never see any of them again ever in life anyway!"

So I got up out of my seat, went outside and picked that dime right off the ground. To my quiet surprise, no one even really paid me any mind. I just went back on the bus and carried on with my day.

That simple action was a declaration to the Universe that I want money in my life and I'm not afraid to grab it when it's offered. Weeks after that, I was blessed with a number of new projects and financial blessings. To this day, if I happen to notice a penny or dime on the ground, I pick it right up. Now I don't go around searching for pennies on the street because my head is held up too high nowadays, but if I do happen to see one shining in the sunlight, I grab it! Don't judge me .

Why Don't You Have Money? Maybe You Don't Know What to Do With It

"Money is like manure, if you pile it all up in one place it stinks, but if you spread it around it makes things grow "

-- Stuart Wilde (1989 seminar)

A lot of us think that when we do get a sum of money, we have to hold onto it tightly. We're so afraid of going back to broke that we still live our lives as if we are broke, holding onto every brown penny.

But that's another message that you're sending out to the Universe—that if you do get some money, you're not going to use it for anything productive or useful. That you won't believe that you're entitled to it and don't even believe that it's real. When you have that mentality, you aren't going to get much more money to "play around" with.

I remember when I suddenly had a spurt of sales of a work that I wrote many years ago. I didn't understand where the spurt came from or how it was happening, but I was getting thousands of dollars each month in sales out of the blue. I didn't even know how to handle the windfall and couldn't believe it was happening. I didn't know what to do with the money—should I invest it, just pay bills or save it? After a month or two, the sales dropped back to a more "realistic" level (at least as far as what I had been conditioned to believe was realistic) and I was upset.

Now I realize exactly what happened. The Universe gave me a demonstration to show me that while I was saying I wanted more money, I wasn't even ready to RECEIVE it when it came. I didn't have any idea or plan for how to use it. You're not going to be given loads of money unless you're planning to MAKE GOOD USE OF IT.

If you look at the average lottery winner who went from "rags to riches," they often go right back to being broke not too long after winning. Why is that? It's because they have absolutely no idea what they're going to do with that immense blessing of cash. In fact, many of them end up even worse off than before. That's not a coincidence—this is the law of attraction (and repulsion) in action. One of my favorite authors Rhonda Byrne made a great point. She said that if you were to split all of the wealth of the world evenly among every person, in a short while all of it would go right back into the hands of the 1% richest families. That's because most people just don't understand how to magnetize money and keep it flowing into their lives.

The $100,000 Question

Author Michael Neill presented a very poignant question in his book Effortless Success. He asked: if you were given $1 million to spend and you had to spend it by the end of the month, what would you spend it on?

I thought about this question and quickly realized that I couldn't even conceive of having $1 million to spend in that short period of time. I had to reduce the amount to $100,000. If that isn't expressive enough of why some of us don't have the millions that we say we want, I don't know what is.

I took the entire day to write down everything I would spend that $100,000 on. That's absolutely ridiculous. Now, if I really wanted a sudden blessing of $100,000 or more, shouldn't I know exactly what I'd use it for?

Well, now I know.

What about you? If someone walked up to you right now and gave you $100,000 (after taxes) to spend on whatever you wanted, what would you spend it on?

I'm working on that million dollar question now. There's a lot that I want to do, and it's up to me to step it up. Imagine having $100 million or even $1 billion to spread around and make things grow.

The $7 Experiment

In 2013 I started a little experimental blog entitled "The $7 Experiment." The purpose of the blog was to prove that when you spread even small amounts of money in the right places, it can yield fruit and blessings that you never even expected. So I focused mainly on investing in projects at DonorsChoose.org, which helps teachers buy the items that they need for their classrooms and young students.

I sowed my first "seed" on 9/2/13 and a day later the project was fully funded. A day after that an old article I posted for sale sold for more than double the amount I donated. I continued this process and financial blessings just kept flowing in. I had proof of something that I'd known all along: when you give from a place of love, you receive. It doesn't make any scientific sense, but it's true nonetheless. My goal in starting the blog was not to "get rich"—it was just to provide evidence that when we put good things out into the world, good things come back.

Money Is Love—Don't Be Afraid to Request What You're Worth

Do you know that most people don't earn what they want to earn simply because they're afraid to ask for it? As a writer, I know this to be true. For some reason, some people don't think that writers are worth paying fairly, even though everything that happens in print, online and television requires a writer. Some copywriters can make $150 to $200 or more per hour. Those copywriters make that kind of money because one day they woke up and said "hey, this is my rate;

take it or leave it." Someone saw their work and agreed to take it.

You have to request what you believe you're worth.

I used to be the type of person who would offer free services to friends and family members. Not anymore. I might offer a small discount, but I need to be paid or compensated in some way for my time and talents.

When you get or give money to someone, it's like you're sharing a form of love. Then you get to spread that love around even more by buying things from other hard working people. You get to help make things grow (remember that metaphor about spreading seeds).

So I strongly suggest that you request fair and reasonable compensation for yourself if you want to thrive in the area of money. That might mean raising your rate if you work for yourself, pricing your products differently or asking for a raise at your current job. If you work hard and offer someone a quality product or service, you have every right to ask for fair compensation in return.

Residual Income Is Key to Thriving

I've saved what I believe to be the most important message about money for last. Despite popular belief, trading time for money (aka working at a job) is not the ideal way to make money. Why? Because it is finite way to make money and you can't get any of the precious time that you spent back.

Most people work at jobs because they believe it is the safest way to live and make money, but it's actually not safe. It's not safe at all. There is no such thing as job security. If you want to ensure that you always have money you must figure out a way to make it on your own.

Residual income is the way to go. It is how people thrive in their financial lives. It is the key to financial freedom. It's making money 24 hours a day—even while you sleep. You don't have to put in any more working hours past the time you took to create the offering or to set up the system to earn that money.

Here's an easy way to approach the idea of residual income when you're just starting out: figure out how to make $150 every month consistently.

Then do it 20 or more times!

When you look at it like that and take action toward making that happen, working a job will seem like less and less of a good use of your time as the months and years progress.

Here are a few common and fairly basic ways to make a residual income:

- becoming an affiliate (Amazon offers a good program) and serving your ads on a website/blog
- writing and selling the usage rights to creative works (for instance a web template if you're a designer or an article if you're a writer)
- creating and selling a movie or music
- writing books that can be delivered online (eBooks, audio, print on demand)
- creating and selling a training program
- creating a web store and setting up a drop ship arrangement with a supplier (they ship on your behalf when an item sells)

Another way to make money without trading your time for money is to hire someone else to spend their time selling something for you while you collect the profit. Guess who does that? Most employers!

Yes, it takes an upfront investment to make some of these things happen, but the investment is often not as extensive as you would think. Maybe you just need to buy a web domain and hire a website designer. You might spend that amount on clothes or entertainment in one month—make a small sacrifice and put it toward your idea.

One of the most difficult parts of creating residual income streams is making a serious and final decision to put the system into action. It takes time, commitment and sometimes a little research to get something set up properly.

Again, if you want financial freedom at some point in your journey, start developing a plan to generate residual income.

"If you don't build your dream someone will hire you to help build theirs."

-- Tony Gaskins Jr.

Part 3: Love and Relationships

I remember that there was a time in my life when I would get on online dating sites trying desperately to meet a new guy. No matter what I did, each encounter with a new guy always ended up the same way and each time it only made me more and more desperate to find someone who would love me and care about me.

Nowadays, I find myself a little overwhelmed by the attention that I receive from men to the point where I don't even know that I have enough time or motivation to pursue a serious relationship with one person at the moment. I am much pickier about who I date and spend time with. I will only settle down with the guy who is right for me in every way.

So what happened between then and now? A whole lot.

Self-Esteem and Confidence Is Key

As a womanist, one of my areas of focus is helping to build self-esteem in women. Having self-esteem and unstoppable confidence is so key to attracting and building a love relationship with a man. I don't know if I can express how important this is in words. It's THE secret to attracting and keeping a man's interest.

A lot of the dating and relationship advice that I give holds value for men as well. It's all about expecting and accepting love, attention, protection, excitement and the "spice of life" into your romantic relationships. All that stuff is what makes a love relationship THRIVE.

So in your dating life or love relationships, I ask, **are you surviving, living or thriving?**

The Fear of Being Alone Is At the Root of All Bad Relationships

A lot of us have a hard time finding real love because we let fear rule over our lives:

- Fear of being alone.
- Fear of your biological clock ticking.
- Fear of family making fun of you or feeling sorry for you because you don't have a husband.
- Fear of feeling like a social misfit around your friends who are in relationships.

- Fear of society judging you as a spinster or the "cat lady."

The list goes on and on. So instead of relaxing and opening ourselves up to love finding us at the right time, many of us actively seek a connection with someone, desperately, like we're on a mission. But when you go after something desperately, you might not like what you find. As they say, be careful what you wish for because you just might get it!

Also, when you go after things desperately, it only attracts more and more stuff to be desperate about!

There was actually a University of Toronto study published in *The Journal of Personality and Social Psychology* that says the fear of being alone is so great that people often choose to be unhappy with the wrong person.

I blogged about how the fear of ending up alone causes many women to end up in bad situations with men.

Blog Post—2/2/14—FWB

The Fear of Ending Up Alone Leads to Bad Choices in Men

When you let the fear of being alone control your dating choices, you tend to rush into situations with guys who you know aren't right for you.

Fear of being alone makes you move an unemployed grown adult man who has a questionable history and multiple children he doesn't support into your house.

Fear of being alone makes you call a guy who slept with you and then didn't call you for weeks to ask for some more mistreatment.

Some women are so afraid of ending up alone with loads of cats as friends that they compromise their self-- respect, dignity and common sense just to be with someone.

You know what's ironic? This type of woman still usually ends up alone in the end after a divorce, being abused, being dumped or experiencing another setback.

Here is the question that all of us ladies must ask ourselves at some point in our lives.

Would I rather be patiently single and have my dignity intact as I grow into my full womanhood, allowing the right people to enter my life

Or

Be in a series of unhappy situations with men throughout life that leave me feeling used up and unfulfilled? Oh yea, and possibly still alone or even *worse* stuck with someone who makes me absolutely miserable?

All because of fear...

When we operate in fear we make really bad choices in men and in life.

So what are the steps to overcome this often debilitating fear that some of us women have about being alone?

1) recognize that you are living in fear
2) spell out the worst case scenario that

you're fearing (like being a cat lady) 3) realize that even if that were to happen, it's not the end of the world! 4) Release the fear and start LIVING your life free and bold with a clear head!

Love Lynn

If you think about it, fear is actually at the root of pretty much all of the bad, rushed and ill-advised decisions that we make in life, including:

- fear of being embarrassed or made fun of
- fear of being ostracized
- fear of being talked about
- fear of being laughed at
- fear of being judged
- fear of appearing weak or vulnerable
- fear of being alone

Here is another piece I wrote that explores how we allow fear to take over and how it can affect our lives when it comes to love and relationships.

Blog Post—9/25/13—FWB Sucks

Why Do Good Girls Finish Last & Bad Girls Get the Guy?

One of the top searched questions that I see are from women who want to know why good girls finish last while bad girls always seem to get the guys.

The answer is really simple: good girls tend to live life fearfully while "bad" girls tend to live life fearlessly.

If you were a guy, which type of woman would you want to be with?

a) A woman who has low self-esteem who is constantly questioning herself and her worth, listening to what everyone tells her to do instead of living in her truth

Or

b) A woman who doesn't care what others thing about her decisions, who is confident, bold and demands what she wants from life? Oh, and she's sexy.

Flip that around if it's hard to grasp—swap out woman for man. Which type of guy would you want to date?

Men Want Bold, Beautiful Women—Even if They're a Little "Trashy" or Mean

It might go against all sense and logic that you've been taught, but most men will choose a "trashy," mean, overtly sexual woman who is bold and confident over a woman who is conservative and afraid to be herself every day of the week.

(By the way, who said these women were "bad" in the first place? The same people who keep you living in fear of judgment every day of your life. Think about that.)

This is not to say that you should become a "bad girl" or start stripping for a living.

It's actually great news, because you can be a good woman who is confident, bold and extremely attractive to men. You can have one up on those so-called "bad" girls, many of whom may one day regret a lot of their decisions.

You don't have to slide down a pole for a living in order to attract men. You just have to:

1) Unconditionally LOVE who you are

2) Have unbending CONFIDENCE in who you are as a woman

3) STOP depending on the opinions of others and FOCUS on your own needs

4) BE BOLD about pursuing what you want in life

5) SPEAK UP for yourself!

You must be a no-nonsense type of woman who gets exactly what she wants from life if you want to be irresistible to men.

It may take a little time to get there after so much brainwashing and negative self-talk, so best to get started today.

Love Lynn

When I let go of my fears related to dating and relationships, it all became so easy. I stopped being fearful of what guys might think of me on a date, where the "relationship" was going and what would happen if I became a lonely spinster with 100 cats.

Remember, fear is **False Evidence Appearing Real**. I know that I'm a smart, resourceful and lovely person with a good personality, so that's probably not going to happen; and even if it did, hey, I really like cats.

Settling Is a Short-Term Solution

As the days, weeks, months and years pass, settling for the first person who comes along starts to seem like more and more of a viable option. You keep relaxing and relaxing your basic standards until they're non-existent, and next thing you know you have a bum living in your house!

Settling is a tempting option but it's only temporary. I wrote about this in a blog post that was inspired by a television show I watched about dating and relationships:

Blog Post—1/7/14—FWB Sucks

I've touched on this point in the past, but I wanted to expand on it. I watched a new show last night < > that inspired these thoughts. In it, one of the women met a man who had been living with his girlfriend for 20 years (I think you might call that a common law marriage, right?) When the cast member found out about it, she was hurt, but shortly after that she moved him into her beautiful NYC apartment.

(Somehow I get the feeling that the 20 year girlfriend wasn't too distraught about him finally moving out!)

I won't judge the cast member, because that is her choice, but I will use this as an example of my point that any woman who really wants to get married or have a relationship can do so quite easily.

When you're willing to drop your standards for the sake of a relationship, you'll find that there are plenty of guys who will want a wife to take care of them (and move into your place) because they haven't been able to take care of themselves in life.

But is that really what you want for your own life? Someone else to take care of just so that you can say you were married?

So this is why I say that any woman who really wants to be married can be married. *Happily* married, not so much.

Always Married, Always Divorced

Have you ever known a woman who always seems to be getting married? She gets out of one bad marriage and six months later she's engaged again?

9 times out of 10 it's because she is one of those women who hasn't set many standards when it comes to men. Getting married and having

a man is all that matters to her in life. She will become ANY man's wife—even if he doesn't have a job, mistreats her, is abusive or has another woman on the side. *And* she will chase him.

There are plenty of men out there who would LOVE to marry a good woman with a job, her own place and plenty of food stocked in her fridge. Of course he needs a car to drive around (and gas money) so that he can impress other women and his friends. Basically, he doesn't have to do anything but exist!

The question is: are YOU as a woman going to be happy in that type of arrangement?

A relationship—especially a marriage—should be reciprocal.

Rocks vs. Gems

In my book *Let Him Chase YOU*, I talk about the difference between "rocks" (men that will hurt you) and "gems" (men that nourish your soul). Let's just say that there seems to be a high rock-to-gem ratio in some places.

Because of this, women of standards may spend a lot of time single compared to women who have thrown standards out of the window, but you have to ask yourself a few serious questions:

Is having a man in your life at all times more important than maintaining your dignity and self-respect as a woman?

Is it worthwhile getting married to a man who you know deep down you'll probably divorce one day? A man who you'll have to support throughout your marriage and maybe even after (men get alimony too)?

I don't think any woman really wants this, but I do understand why some women fall into this trap. I get it—it's hard navigating this world alone sometimes, but it's even harder doing it with someone who could make your life more challenging than it needs to be.

Love Lynn

I wrote about settling again after hearing that a study estimated that 73 percent of people who are currently in relationships are settling for their partners. 73 percent!

Blog Post—10/8/13—FWB Sucks

73% of People in Relationships Are Settling

A survey of people in relationships revealed that 73% of paired people admit that they are just settling for the person they're with.

They're just biding their time. They're just "making due."

That's pretty sad.

To add to that, 17% of people meet their soul mate when it's too late, because they were so eager to just be married or paired up for these reasons:

- pressure from friends and family

- wanting their partner's money

- afraid of being alone

- want the dramatics and attention of a wedding

But they don't achieve true happiness in their unions.

Soul mates Exist

On the same television show < > the guests talked about meeting your soul mate.

Soul mates are real. I know, because I met one of mine.

A soul mate is someone you have an undeniable connection with. You meet and NEITHER of you want to part. Nothing and no one can keep you apart. You don't have to debate or wonder how to approach or "flirt" with that person because you're going to run right into them in some way. You're drawn together. You have the feeling that you've met that person before, almost as if you've known them forever.

Some believe that there are "soul groups"—people who when you find them you all connect in an unimaginable way and have an amazing life experience together, whether they're friends, business partners or your romantic partner.

Back to That 73% Figure

Knowing these honest feelings from people in relationships, if you're a single person do you really feel the need to rush into a relationship with someone?

As I explain in my guide, *Let Him Chase YOU*, it's important to limit your time with people who are in unfulfilling relationships when you are on a mission to find your true love. That's because paired up people who are settling will:

a) make you feel bad about being alone

b) try to pair you up with someone who may not be right for you (so that you can settle too)

c) put you on a negative energy level that isn't right for attracting your soul mate into your life

Do you believe your soul mate is out there and waiting to meet you? If you do, like I do, don't block that person from entering your life by filling it with someone you're just settling for.

Love Lynn

Demand What You Want, and You'll Eventually Get It

Many women don't realize the power that they have when it comes to relationships. If you make demands and focus on what you DO want in a relationship, eventually it will come to you.

But again, you have to be ***very clear*** about what you ask for when you make a request, and that encompasses every aspect of your life.

Many women are afraid to demand what they want from a relationship because they're afraid that the guy will consider her a bitch or leave her alone.

I'm not really talking about demanding diamonds and material things (though if that's what you really want from a relationship, go for it). What I'm really talking about is basic respect. It's reasonable to demand that someone shows respect for you. It's reasonable to demand acknowledgment. It's reasonable to demand consideration from another person who wants to be in your life.

If that other person can't deal with the fact that you're a woman with high self-esteem and standards, who demands what she needs and wants out of life, he's not the person that YOU need in your life. Release that person immediately!

But here's the rub—in order to get the respect that you want from others, you have to respect yourself first.

And to be clear, as I explained in *Let Him Chase You,* there's a difference between being a woman who is in control of herself and a woman who tries to control everyone else. You can't *force* anyone to do anything, but you can demand that they treat you right IF they want to be in your life.

Here's a blog post that I wrote about this.

Blog Post—7/31/13—FWB Sucks

Women and Dating: Demand Exactly What You Want from a Relationship

Golden relationship advice: Request exactly what you want and need, and not what you think someone ELSE wants or needs.

Sounds simple enough, right?

But countless women across America and beyond frequently settle for relationships, or rather "arrangements" with men that offer little to none of what they want or need.

They do it mostly because they think that is what the guy will want, or that it is all they are worthy of.

What Exactly Are You Afraid Of?

When you settle for an unfulfilling relationship and don't demand what you want and need from a guy, what are you afraid of?

That he will not want the same thing? If he doesn't you're just not dealing with the right guy. "Toss the rock" over your shoulder and keep yourself open to other options.

We women have a bad tendency to settle on one guy too soon and too easily. You may be surprised at the results when you pull away and keep meeting people instead of settling for someone who can't give you what you want and need.

Are you living your life in fear of being alone to the point where you would accept any treatment or excuse for a relationship?

Please stop doing that. It only matters if you're BOTH happy.

You deserve better.

Love Lynn

Do You Really Really Really Want a Relationship Right Now?

As someone who has been engaged in a serious relationship before, I know how difficult it can be. It isn't always like the perfect, easy relationships you see in movies or television shows. You may have to give up little pieces of yourself to accommodate this new person in your life. You have to think about someone else's needs along with your own. You have to call him when you go out with your friends to let him know that you're all right. If you want to backpack across Europe for a month, you're going to have to convince your significant other that this is a good idea. If you live with someone, you're going to have to deal with all of their quirks and annoyances.

My late fiancé used to have the worst kitchen habits. He would cook a beautiful meal, but then leave the stove full of dirty pots and pans. I do not like dirty dishes. When he did wash the dishes, he would use the same sponge that he used to wipe out a greasy pan to clean a glass! It was a huge pet peeve of mine, to the point where I bought a special sponge and hung it up far away from the sink. We would get into arguments about this silly type of stuff all of the time.

This is just a minor example of the way you have to compromise when you're in a relationship. What about when your significant other has children from a previous relationship? What if he loses his job and you have to take up the slack in your marriage? Are you prepared for all of that?

When you agree to a serious relationship, you're taking on a whole new set of behaviors, habits and issues into your life. Make sure that this is what you really want because you want it for YOU and not for someone else. Make sure that you're not jumping into a relationship just because you can't stand being alone.

Part 4: Your Family & Other Relationships

At this point in my life, I certainly don't need anyone to tell me that family members can be very influential. They can be a force of good or a force that makes you struggle continually in your life. These are the people who you've grown up with since you were a child. These are the people who saw you born. These are the people with whom you've celebrated birthday after birthday. That's a major bond that has formed over the years.

And unfortunately, they can also be the people who will hold you back from achieving major things in your life.

I am focusing on family in this particular book because I believe that if you can learn how to manage and handle your difficult relationships with family members, you can handle just about anyone in your life! That includes friends, associates, co-workers and significant others.

So here's that question again: **are you surviving, living or thriving when it comes to your relationships with your family members and close loved ones?**

Family Members and Those Close to You May Be Implanting Negativity in Your Life

When I went through a very stressful time in my life, I had to learn the hard way that no one, including my family members, was going to come to my rescue. In my mind I imagined that someone would show up on my doorstep one day with flowers or a pound cake and drink coffee with me as I poured out my feelings. They would hug me and let me know that everything would be alright.

But that didn't happen. Not one person in my life checked in on me or came to see me for many months.

I used to be angry about this, but I no longer hold onto resentment about it for three important reasons:

> 1) It taught me how to save *myself*
>
> 2) It made me realize that I shouldn't care so much about how others perceive me and what I choose to do in my life. The negative judgments of others don't feed or nourish me and
>
> 3) I can now admit that it was partly my fault. I refused to open up to anyone to

> let them know that I really needed some help in the first place. I just assumed they would know.

When I renewed my life and finally started on the right path, I came back around some of my family members and slowly began to realize that some of them were the source of a lot of the stress and drama that I had allowed to rule over my life for many years.

Family members are often the main carriers of negativity into your life as you take steps toward THRIVING. They can hold you back by re-implanting those limiting beliefs in your mind (I talked about those in the first part), by passing their personal issues over to you, or by constantly ridiculing your dreams so that you won't seriously try to pursue them.

There are so many reasons why a family member or close relative might do this to you, and it's not always malicious. One of the most common reasons is that they just don't want to lose you. They know that if you achieve a certain level of success, you will probably leave them and they won't be able to reach you anymore. Or maybe they fear for your safety.

Some family members will discourage you because they are allowing their own limiting beliefs and views of the world to not only cloud their minds, but also to affect yours.

The message in all of this is that you can't always assume that just because someone is your family member or someone very close to you that they have *your* best interests in mind. If someone is for your best interests, they will encourage you to pursue your dreams and lift you up no matter what.

Here is a blog post that I wrote immediately after watching a documentary on television about the superstar marathon swimmer Diana Nyad, who made a historic swim from Cuba to Florida.

Blog Post—1/1/14—Life Love Lynn

The Negative Voices around You: The Other Shore: The Diana Nyad Story

I finally had a chance to watch The Other Shore: The Diana Nyad Story documentary. She is the lady who planned a swim from Cuba to Florida. This documentary was a perfect example of how the negative people around you can hold you back from accomplishing things in life.

One person close to Diana was negative about her swim from start to finish. She told Diana she couldn't do it before, during and after her historic attempts to swim from Cuba to Florida.

In some cases people will discourage you because of their own personal fears.

In other cases it's jealousy and insecurity because they don't have the guts to accomplish anything real in life.

Back to the documentary, I believe this person in Diana's life was just really frightened about losing her loved one. And that is understandable.

But regardless of her motivations, it's still a problem when you have a demotivating person in your life who is constantly telling you that you can't do something.

They can't see what you see—all that they can see is the circumstances right in front of them. They can't dream like you—yet.

Sometimes that negative person's will and energy is so strong that they can interrupt, intercept or delay your goals. In Diana's case, what she needed was a BOOST when she hit those milestones. All that she got was fear, doubt and negativity from some of the people around her.

Diana's case was extreme because her life was in danger for her dreams. But for most of us, our dreams are attainable without having to risk our lives. Yet some of us still don't take the chance because we have negative people around us telling us that we can't. We're scared of social disapproval and people saying "I told you so." We care too much about the opinions of other people when it comes to our dreams and goals.

So who do you have in YOUR life that is holding you back from your ultimate accomplishment? You may find that removing that voice from your life might be the one way to open a road toward meeting or achieving your long time goal—and it could happen more quickly than you ever imagined.

Love Lynn

Here is another post that I wrote when I was feeling weary and conflicted after spending the holidays around some family members. Since then, I have resolved those feelings and some of the conflicts I experienced with the people in my life, but I still feel that the message here is valid for people who think they may have toxic people in their lives.

Blog Post—11/30/13—FWB SUCKS

Are You Allowing Toxic Family Members to Take Up Space in Your Life?

I blog often about the transformation I made in my life. I experienced improvement in every area from fulfillment in my work to better relationships.

Now that my mind is clearer I'm coming to some harsh realizations. One thing I am learning is that just because someone is related to you by blood doesn't necessarily mean that they have to be in your life.

This Thanksgiving holiday I witnessed some things about some of the people I am closely related to that has me seriously asking—do I really need to have someone in my life just because we're related?

I don't think so.

The behavior—selfishness, lack of consideration, lack of gratitude just to name a few—is certainly nothing new to me. But for some reason this particular holiday is the first time I am seriously considering that certain folks might be toxic in my life and not good for my personal growth. I felt some old feelings, thoughts and resentments come back that definitely don't have any place in my new life!

Negative Energy Is Contagious

Do you have someone like this in your family? Someone who you feel forced to be around just because they are blood relations? Someone who lacks consideration for you and others? Someone who brings down your energy?

The energy that you have around you is important. Negative energy is highly contagious so you should make every effort to keep it away from you. If someone makes you feel upset, angry or disgusted every time you see them, maybe you shouldn't be around that person at all—even if they're related to you. Give them a chance to experience their own personal growth before allowing them back into your life. Nothing should hold you back from growing.

As you make your own transformations in your life and in your relationships, I think it's important to consider whether you are holding onto some people solely out of a sense of familial obligation and allowing them to infiltrate your life with negative energy.

It may be necessary to cut those "ties that bind" (at least temporarily) in order to allow better relationships and experiences into your world.

Love Lynn

One of my favorite motivational speakers, Les Brown, tells stories about how some of his family members were the main ones rooting for him to fail. His own twin brother would taunt him whenever he experienced a setback, telling Les that he was a dreamer for wanting to be a motivational speaker and a rich business man. They told him he should go back and get a job at a department store. They told him that he might as well give up on all of that "nonsense" he was working on.

Well of course, Les became a huge success known the world over, earning tens of thousands of dollars in appearance fees, and proved everyone wrong. His story is a perfect example of how important it is to filter negative family members and "friends" out of your life as you take steps toward greatness.

For a long time the people around me would ask me "why don't you go back to the corporate world." They just could not grasp my dream of working for myself. They planted a lot of self-doubt in my mind over the years, but I still stuck to my plan and continued developing my business.

Now here's a question that you might find difficult to answer honestly right now. And that's okay, but at least think about it:

Are YOU one of these negative people? Have you been discouraging someone you love from going after their goals and dreams? You can't expect unconditional love, support and encouragement from other people if you don't offer it yourself. We sometimes find it easy to convict others of wrongdoing against us, but have a hard time admitting when we do it to others.

The point here is that we all have to be careful about the things that we say to the people we love. They need our support and encouragement; not our judgment and seeds of doubt.

Don't Let People Bait You into Fights

"Never argue with a fool, onlookers may not be able to tell the difference."

--- Mark Twain

You don't have to attend every argument you're invited to.

-- Author Unknown

Some people can literally make your blood boil. They come around you and make snide or snarky remarks. They bring up negative things from the past. When this happens, you can actually feel something rise up in you physically. The next thing you know, you're engaged in an all-out war of the words—maybe even an altercation.

There are people who just love to fight. They love conflict and thrive off of it, because that's all that they know. These types of people will try to bait you into a fight—please don't let them.

People who love to fight and argue know exactly what to say to trigger you to flip out. As I like to say, they go for the jugular—they try to get that "dagger" in there and turn and twist it to *really* hurt your feelings.

And when they do this, they are expecting you to jump back at them with anger in response. When you do this, they know they have you right where they want you: down in the mud getting dirty with them.

If you've ever watched a reality television show, you can tell that the casting directors carefully pick certain types of people—people who don't know how to manage their feelings and are always ready for a showdown. They are hurt people who are always ready to hurt other people when necessary.

The best thing you can do when someone tries to bait you into an argument with ugly or fighting words is to remain calm, smile or laugh at them and leave their presence.

You see, that person is prepared for you to fight her back verbally, but she isn't prepared for you to laugh at her and tell her to have a good day.

When people try to bait me into arguments, I'll admit that it is still difficult to resist jumping down their throats (as I would do in the past). It really takes everything in you to remain calm. But it is so much more rewarding than giving them what they want—a fight, argument, stress, drama, more anger and more hurt feelings being spread around.

Don't Take Things So Personally

If you can learn not to take the things that people say and do so personally, you will have a much more fun and drama-free life. Being able to heartily laugh at people (outwardly or inwardly) when they try to insult you is extremely powerful.

When someone says something to or about me that I feel is judgmental and meant to hurt my feelings, I smile to myself and sometimes picture a "Do I Give a Damn What You Think?" meter in my mind, struggling to move from zero. That makes me laugh. The Do I Give a Damn meter rarely moves much these days, and that's alright with me.

All of this is much easier to do when you genuinely stop caring so much about what other people think of you (I'll discuss this more in the next section on self-love).

Your family members and people closest to you know the most about you, which is why their words often hurt the worst. They will bring up a situation that happened 15 years ago that you just want to go away. Or they'll tease you about a trait that they know you're sensitive about. So as I said, if you can learn how to stay cool around your family, you can handle just about anyone.

Hurt People Hurt People

Here's a secret—when someone says something judgmental or hurtful to you, **they're really**

talking about themselves. I repeat: when someone says something disrespectful, judgmental or hurtful to you, they are talking about themselves and don't even realize it. They are expressing their own personal insecurities, fear and lack of self-worth in the only way that they know how to—by transferring it onto other people.

Here's an example. As a writer and blogger who has been publishing my works to the world for years, I had to learn how to manage criticisms of my work and keep writing anyway!

For instance, when I wrote my first dating guide for women entitled *Friends with Benefits Sucks,* I sent out review copies. One beautiful morning months later I woke up with the birds chirping outside my window and a smile on my face. I picked up my phone and was greeted with an unfriendly email from a reviewer, telling me how much she hated the book and that she was giving it 1-star. Her review was long and she didn't have one positive thing to say about it.

Now as a side note, I don't think that I've ever given anything a 1-star review. I don't think I ever would unless the book was complete gibberish or full of hate. I don't even consider 1-star reviews in my decisions to buy new books because they seem so personal.

So I immediately realized that this person was probably hurting about something, maybe even feeling convicted by something written in the book, and instead of dealing with her personal issues she chose to try to hurt someone else. I simply responded with a thank you and moved on with my day. It's not an easy thing for a writer to do, but I have learned that it just isn't productive to let negativity rule over your day.

People who are happy and love themselves don't feel the need to constantly judge, make fun of, gossip about and look down on other people. People who are miserable and unhappy do this. Passing negative comments and attitudes to others gives miserable people the only (temporary) joy that they can possibly feel in their day. You have to understand this.

If you can remember this truth the next time someone says or does something hurtful to you, you might even find yourself sympathizing with them instead of feeling bad about yourself.

One quick side note: be aware of those who need to put another person's work, style or essence down in order to lift *themselves* up.

Saying NO (And Loving It)

If you were brought up how I was brought up, saying no to others (especially as a woman) was like a foreign concept. We're supposed to put our own happiness, sanity and security on the line, after all, for the sake of others.

But as I grew older, I started to embrace the NO in me. It's that part of me that says "hell no, you can't borrow $20 from me." The part that says, "hell no, you can't have sex with me then not call me for weeks." The part of me that said "hell no, you're not going to talk to me that way and think that it's okay with me."

And I love that part of me. Now, other people might not like it so much, but their opinion doesn't hold much weight when it comes to what is good for ME.

In the past, I would fear (there goes that word again) what other people might think of me if said NO to their requests. These days, I almost revel in the chance at telling someone NO when they ask me something that I find unreasonable. My time, my well-being, my money and my sanity matters more than your request.

And what I have found is that, nothing really changes in your relationship with people when you tell them NO, except that they don't call you asking for stuff anymore! If it's a family member, he will still talk to you at Thanksgiving dinner. If it's a friend, she will still have fun with you on girl's night out. If it's a "romantic" interest, he will probably respect you even more for telling him what he needs to hear: NO.

Here's a blog post that I wrote about the importance of using that beautiful two-lettered word NO when necessary (especially for women):

Blog Post—8/13/13—FWB Sucks

Learn to Say NO, Even If It Might Hurt Someone's Feelings

I was once faced with a tough decision regarding someone who I worked with. I made a commitment to perform a job, but matters arose that would make it impossible.

I spent nights not sleeping, worrying about how I would break the news to this person who was counting on me (and who I really like as a person by the way).

All in all, I was worried about how I would tell this person "no." No, I can't do it.

I finally did say no, and as hard as it may have been, was it really necessary to do all of that worrying in the meantime? How many hours did I waste worrying about something that was essentially out of my control?

Putting Your Needs First
Sometimes situations arise where you have to put your needs before the needs or wants of someone else. Keeping this in mind is ultra-important when you are dating men.

A lot of us women are people-pleasers. We don't want to hurt feelings or disappoint people.

So when a guy suggests that you have sex way too soon, or asks you to pick him up and drive him around, or asks you to perform some other inappropriate action, you are afraid to say no for fear of disappointing him or losing him.

That's no way to conduct your dating life if you want to be taken seriously as a woman. If it isn't right, you MUST say no even if it will displease the guy you're dating.

What you'll probably find is that the guy will respect you MORE when you stand up for yourself and say no.

Make a Decision and Stick with It

The next time you are faced with a decision about a guy (or just in life in general) give yourself some time to ponder what the right choice is.

Then, make a firm decision and stick to it. Do not waver and do not worry about what the other person will say or think if you must say NO.

Even if it might disappoint the other person, when you say no, ask yourself this question: How much would it disappoint, inconvenience or hurt YOU if you were to say yes?

Love Lynn

Love Them No Matter What

"I have decided to stick with love. Hate is too great a burden to bear."

-- Martin Luther King, Jr.

No matter how much the people around you stress you out or cause you frustration, you have to love them ANYWAY. Love is the solution. Love is the source and the power. Love is the answer to every problem in our lives.

You can't fight negativity with anger, hate or more negativity. Doing that only brings you more of the same. You can only get rid of a dark room by adding light.

But love doesn't mean that you have to be around someone 24 hours a day trying to help them or putting up with a lot of negativity. Sometimes the best way to show someone love is to step away, pray or meditate and give the relationship time to heal. As I mentioned earlier, sometimes the best way to show someone love is to tell them NO.

It helps to clarify your feelings, and at the same time tell the truth about your feelings... For instance:

I might not agree with you, but I still love you.

I might not like what you just said to me, but I still love you.

I might not like your face right now, but I still love you.

Also, try to put yourself in the other person's shoes. What do they see when they look at you? Maybe the problem doesn't just lie in THEIR behavior—maybe there are a few things YOU can work on too. I do this self-reflection if I find myself in a conflict with someone close to me that I don't understand. What could I be doing or saying to cause this person to feel hurt or slighted?

Gratitude

As many things may be going wrong in your relationships with family members and the people closest to you, you can probably think of at least a few things that they have done or said to you in the past that were really wonderful.

This may sound hard to do, but FOCUS ON THOSE THINGS whenever you think about them. If you do this consistently it is easier and easier to envelop them in feelings and thoughts of love—even if you can't be around them at the moment. Again, remember that hurt people hurt people, so if you feel that someone is constantly attacking you it's probably because they are unhappy or troubled themselves. Sympathize with them instead of hating or fighting with them.

As you're working toward thriving in your life, you simply can't allow anger and resentment to hold you back from your blessings. Gratitude and love is the key.

Part 5: Self-Love

Love yourself first and everything else falls into line. You really have to love yourself to get anything done in this world.

-- Lucille Ball

Though I ordered this part about self-love last, it really comes first. There is no exception to this rule no matter which way you try to slice it. You have to love yourself first and foremost.

Even if someone does manage to achieve some level of success in life while hating his or herself, it can't last for very long. I'm a firm believer that self-love is crucial to THRIVING in every other area of your life.

So are you just barely surviving, living or thriving when it comes to loving yourself? Let's talk about this some more—a whole lot more, because it's so important.

You Express Your Love or Hate for Yourself Every Day in Every Way

What's your self-talk like? In other words, when you're all by yourself and lost in your thoughts, how do you talk to yourself?

Do you lift yourself up with encouragement and tell yourself that things are getting better and better in your life every day?

Or do you tell yourself how stupid you are and how unloved you are and how ugly you are?

Do you make yourself laugh and smile with your thoughts, or do you make yourself cry?

You're unconsciously talking to yourself all day long. Your mind might be playing tricks on you. And it may be holding you back from opportunities.

I was very shy as a young girl. I've always been more of a reserved and reflective sort of person, lost in my thoughts. So I never seriously considered taking a job in sales until it was a necessity. I was nervous about selling to people in a face to face situation or over the phone --- why would they want to buy from me?

But then one day I jumped in and started selling. I sold more than any of the other trainees. In another selling situation I managed to sell hundreds of dollars in product in about two hours.

I quickly learned that sales is more about selling *yourself* than selling a product. If I had continued to listen to my negative self-talk about being too shy to sell to people, I might not have learned that I am actually a natural saleswoman.

Words Hurt; but We Control How They Will Affect Our Lives

A lot of the hate or anger that some of us feel comes from messages that we've received over the years from our family members, peers, so-called friends, associates, bosses, spouses and lovers.

There's that boy in school who harassed you daily and said you were the ugliest thing he had ever seen in his life. There was that family member who told you that you wouldn't ever amount to much and that parent who sang the praises of your sister or brother while ignoring you.

They say that sticks and stones may break your bones but words can never hurt you. Well guess what, sticks and stones may hurt but physical wounds heal relatively quickly. Emotional wounds last and last and in some cases they can leave a hole in your soul that makes it hard for you to accept love into your heart.

I wrote about the power of words in a blog post:

Blog Post -- 12/7/13—FWB Sucks

Whoever Said Words Can Never Hurt... Lied!

From the time we were kids we were taught the saying:

"Sticks and stones may break bones but words will never hurt me"

I don't know who came up with that saying; maybe someone with good intentions who was trying to help, but it's a lie nonetheless.

Words hurt. They can cut DEEP and leave scars that don't always heal with time.

How else can you explain someone who is 40 years old and still hurt about being teased or shunned in high school? How else do you explain a person living a limited, unhappy life just because someone told them they wouldn't amount to anything?

A number of recent events in my own life have shown me the true power of words, how they can really hurt and how they can sit on a person's soul for years and years—sometimes even a lifetime.

When someone tells a child that "sticks and stones" line they're assuming that the child is strong enough to resist the ugliness of those words. Not all children are—some children are fragile and don't have high self-esteem. They need more training and more encouragement at home to be able to prevent internalizing those hurtful words for years into the future.

A Better Saying...

I think the better saying would be that words may hurt you, but you shouldn't let them DEFINE you.

You can't deny that when someone says something hurtful to you, it stings. But the strength is in taking that insult in the proper context and then REJECTING it completely.

This is the proper context: people who try to hurt you with their words are reflecting their own hurt out into the world. The way they choose to deal with their own pain is to try to make someone else feel worse. They get a fleeting satisfaction from that (keyword: fleeting).

It's up to each one of us to recognize this so that we can better let those ugly utterances bounce right off of us like Jell-O, knowing that it has no basis in reality. Its real basis is in anger, emotional pain and confusion.

So let's repeat this new affirmation to ourselves and to the young people in our lives: words might hurt you, but you can't let them DEFINE you.

"To be yourself in a world that is constantly trying to make you something else is the greatest accomplishment."

-- Ralph Waldo Emerson

Love Lynn

Some people just love to try to hurt others with their words, don't they? But regardless of their intentions, we are the ones who give them power by paying them attention and giving validation to their comments. You have to learn to laugh at negative people (and also to teach the children in our lives to do this to their bullies). You have to put them in their "proper place" mentally without reacting to them.

You Matter

Why is it that you think so much of the people around you, but don't value yourself as a smart, thinking, feeling human people in need of love just like everyone else? Why is it that you want to help everyone else but refuse to offer assistance to YOURSELF?

Blog Post—3/1/14—Life Love Lynn

You Can't Be Everything to Everyone... Especially If You're Nothing to Yourself

Why is it that some of us think so much of others but not much of ourselves?

Maybe because we've allowed so many negative messages about ourselves to enter our heads over the years since childhood, but for some reason we don't think anyone else could have had the same experience.

In our minds, everyone else is living well and oh so happy. Everyone else is just great! But we can't see the greatness in ourselves.

The truth is that everyone else around us is probably going through the same stuff. But because we think everyone ELSE is awesome and perfect, we will do more for them and pay more attention to them than our own selves. How twisted is that?

Women do this the most by far.

Do you downgrade yourself when talking about yourself but uplift and support everyone else?

Are you always coming to the rescue of others but don't think you're worthy or important enough to help yourself?

Do you minimize your own light to let the light of others to shine brighter?

This can apply to something as seemingly minor as neglecting to tell people that it's your birthday. Are you the type of person who will hold back from telling people that it's your birthday, on the day of your birthday, for fear of seeming "narcissistic" or self-serving? I used to be one of those people, but now I am more than happy to tell everyone who will listen that it's my b-day or that it's coming up soon. Yes! This was the day that the awesome human being that is ME came to be. Celebrate with me baby!

And guess what? I get gifts, birthday wishes and special dinner offers when I do that!

So here is the question of this post:

How can you be everything to everyone else when you're nothing to yourself?

The answer is that you can't. No way possible. Even people who have sky high self-esteem and self-worth know that it's impossible to please or help everyone.

Take care of yourself! I can't stress this enough. It's admirable to want to help others but it's only truly EFFECTIVE when you're mentally, emotionally, physically and financially healthy first.

Love Lynn

This is another post that I wrote when I was feeling very strongly about a story of a girl who ended her life, presumably over relationship drama:

Blog Post—9/10/13—FWB Sucks

Self-Love and Feeling Like You Don't Matter

"She always had a big heart for everybody, but not for herself."

An episode of Dr. Phil caught my attention. His guest was the mother of a young woman who cut her own life short because she was unhappy about relationships.

Something her lovely mother said in the beginning of the show caught my attention. She said of her deceased daughter, "She always had a big heart for everybody, but not for herself."

This is a very tragic case that demonstrates the importance of SELF-love. How can a person have and show so much love for everyone else in her life, but not for her own self?

What makes everyone else worthy of love and not yourself?

I believe that it partially stems from childhood issues and is then exasperated by adult issues.

What the mother said struck me because I have been there. Feelings of being unworthy, unloved and unimportant. For me I believe it stemmed from being ignored and teased as a child and also being taught that as a girl I should always put the needs of others before my own. Mothers unconsciously teach this to their girls all of the time.

In this case her mother confirmed that her father's abandonment was the source of her despair and feelings of being unwanted.

What to Do?

If you can admit that you have similar feelings of being useless, unloved and unimportant, the first step is identifying where this came from.

That person who told you that was LYING. They were miserable or STUCK themselves, so they took it out on you instead of resolving their own personal issues.

Once you are clear on the source of these dangerous thoughts swimming around in your head, the next step is SHOUTING THEM DOWN whenever they talk to you. They whisper in your ear ever so gently like a snake. When they start up, say it out loud if need be: YOU LIE! YOU ARE A LIAR!

You DO matter. You are loved and you are loveable. I don't even know you but I love you, that's why I'm writing this to you, so there you go!

You DO have a purpose here in this world, and that's why you're still here.

I Understand

I know what you're going through—not very long ago I was curled up in a ball in my bed, in the dark, covers over my head, completely alone, with my cellphone turned off, for months, wondering why I even existed.

If I hadn't come out of that, I wouldn't be here right now, reaching you with uplifting words of love. I wouldn't have had the inspiration to write two new books and revive my business. My life is better simply because my thoughts are better. I have a purpose and so do you, even if it doesn't seem that way right now.

When people unfortunately cut their lives short they do a great disservice to the entire universe because they don't get a chance to live out that purpose. Don't let those negative thought patterns take control over your life. You're special and you're meant to be here.

That alone is enough to justify loving every bit of who you are—a being perfectly crafted by God.

Start shouting down those thoughts of being unloved, unworthy, ugly or unimportant right now, don't waste another moment.

I Love You

Lynn

Being Alone Is the Best Time to Get to Know YOU

Living alone is sometimes difficult, but it can be a huge blessing. You don't have anyone to worry about, feed or think about on a day to day basis except for yourself.

It is also a great time to get in touch with yourself and learn more about what makes you tick.

I used the time that I spent isolated from family and loved ones to figure out why I was experiencing the same situations over and over again.

As author Cherie Carter-Scott explains in her book *If Life Is a Game, These Are the Rules,* it's because we haven't yet learned a lesson.

For instance, if we keep having the same experience in our relationships, it's probably because we haven't learned that we're going for the wrong type of guy. If we have the same problem at every job that we start, it's some habit that we're taking from place to place that's causing the same results.

I think that spending quality alone time with yourself is the best way to come to terms with what's happening in your life and what *has* been happening in your life for years.

Some people choose to use this time to get very detailed about who and what caused them to be in the predicament that they are in, while others use this time to explore how they themselves caused their own problems.

Of course, the people who take responsibility are the people who ultimately win. Once you take full responsibility for your life, good things start to happen for you. I talk more about this at the end.

Here is a blog post that I wrote about using time alone to get stronger:

Blog Post—12/20/13—FWB Sucks

Feeling Alone: When You're All You've Got, That's More Than Enough

One of the most difficult yet powerful experiences you can have is finding yourself in a position where the only person on this earth you can count on or call on is YOU.

I went through this experience after losing someone who was very near and dear to me. It was extremely difficult to go from talking to this friend every day to not talking at all.

What hurt even more was when my phone went completely silent and I didn't hear from anyone for weeks at a time. Now THAT is an eye opening experience.

But even in the midst of the disappointment and loneliness, somehow I knew that it was an important learning experience. It was something I had to go through. I constantly heard that little voice within tell me that it was going to be okay; that I needed to go through this to prove to myself that I could make it on my own. That I had to stop relying on the support or approval of others to get by in life. That all I had to do was trust in God—even if no one on this earth is there for me, God is with me always.

It took some time but I slowly picked myself up and pushed forward. Even though I felt as if I was crumbling inside each day, I went to work at a new job where no one knew me. I smiled (even when I wanted to cry) and eventually became one of the best workers there. I kept pushing on.

I listened to motivational speakers, like Les Brown and Napoleon Hill who told me that I am in total control of my destiny. That my own negative thoughts and beliefs were what was holding me back from happiness.

Slowly but surely I started to become myself again until I finally pulled myself completely out of that dark place. I started back on my path even more refreshed and motivated than ever. And I did it all on my own! That is so powerful.

If you're going through a similar experience where you feel completely alone and like you're all you've got in this world, this may just be an important lesson—a lesson that if learned could empower you throughout your life.

Even if you feel like you're all you've got in the world, you've got to convince yourself that you're enough. You don't need someone else to come to your rescue—step up, take responsibility for your life and SAVE YOURSELF!

Love Lynn

Prioritizing Your Needs

Do you believe that your own needs are important? Or do you allow the needs and requests of others to take precedence over your own? Think about it.

There's a saying that you have to make sure that your oxygen mask is on before you try to help someone else in distress. How can you effectively help others if you're not well, healthy and happy yourself? There's no shame or fault in prioritizing your own needs before you try to come to the assistance of others.

Here's a blog post that I wrote on this topic:

Blog Post—1/24/14—Life Love Lynn

Yes I Matter, I Come First, and What?: Prioritizing Your Needs as a Woman

As a young girl and woman I was always the one who selflessly gave of myself to others—even when it wasn't convenient for me. I'd take the smallest portion to eat, even though I had just spent hours in the kitchen cooking the meal. I would relinquish a spot at the outlet in a coffee shop so that someone else could charge up, even if that meant I would have to cut my time working or studying short. I would go out of my way to please men sexually, even when I wasn't really pleased in return. I would drive people all around town to help them out even if it caused me to be late for my own affairs.

I think a lot of us women do these things in one way or another—putting others ahead of us; putting their needs ahead of ours. It's a learned behavior—a lot of us learn it from watching the older women in our families do this 24/7 for years and years.

For me that type of thinking is now a distant memory as I have adopted the new motto: "I am the most important person in my life." I believe that statement should be true in every person's life.

This is not a call for us to be selfish and neglect everyone around us—it's a call for us to stop being selfless as women and prioritize our own needs. Being selfless is not good—we NEED self. We need that self to be strong and happy. The truth is that if we're not okay, we can't do much good for anyone else. This includes mothers, wives, caregivers, employees and volunteers. It's crucial that we tend to our own needs first and foremost—only then can we properly tend to the DESERVING AND APPRECIATIVE people on our lives who need our help and provide reciprocal support/love.

So if someone tries to make you feel guilty for putting your needs before theirs, don't be afraid to stand up and say "YES I MATTER, I COME FIRST IN MY LIFE. Who comes first in YOUR life?"

Showing love and attention to yourself is one of the first bold steps toward complete and unlimited happiness. Start today.

Love Lynn

Here is another post that I wrote going into more detail about why being selfless is actually not a positive or admirable trait:

Blog Post—2/1/14—Life Love Lynn

3 Reasons Why Being Selfless Is Actually Pretty Selfish

A quick search of the definition of selflessness turns up this result: "Having, exhibiting or motivated by no concern for oneself."

In other words, being selfless is like trying to be a martyr. You sacrifice your needs in favor of others. You don't care about yourself (or at least you say you don't), only others.

Some believe that this term is synonymous with being unselfish, but I disagree. Let me tell you why I think being selfless is actually a very selfish way to live.

1. It Creates a Vacuum.

Being selfless is not normal. It basically says that everyone else in the world is important except for you. But you should be the most important person in your life. You are an important being. So when you go about your life with this attitude it's like you're creating a sort of vacuum where positive energy (your positive life force) is constantly being sucked out of you but you're not allowing it to be replaced. When someone does come to you and say "let me help you" the "selfless" attitude within causes you to say "No no no. I don't need help. I don't need love. I don't deserve or want any of that goodness." You're rejecting the good from coming back into your life, which is making it harder for the Universe to do its job. The Universe doesn't like that—it wants you to be filled up to the brim and beyond with good things. *Fighting natural laws is selfish.*

2. It Demands Recognition.

When you selflessly spread yourself thin by preoccupying yourself with the lives of others, in a way it is a cry for attention, love and recognition. You believe that if you do everything for everybody, one day the world will say "Man, that Sally is just so awesome!" Then when that doesn't happen as you dreamed it would, and people just start to expect you to help them out all of the time, you become resentful and angry. *Constantly putting yourself out on a limb because you want to be seen as a modern day martyr is selfish.*

3. **You're Ignoring Your Own Needs.**

When you're selfless, you're actually being the most selfish to YOURSELF. You have needs just like the next person. You matter just like the next person. So if you run yourself ragged every day helping everyone else and don't even stop to nourish your own mind, body and soul you are doing a great disservice to yourself. You are the only person who you can really count on to take care of your needs. *Ignoring your own needs is being selfish to yourself.*

When you think about it from this perspective, clearly being selfish and selfless are negative behaviors. A happy, healthy and fulfilled person is open to helping others but not at the expense of her own sanity and well-being.

Do your daily behaviors fall under the category of being "selfless?"

If so, it may be time to re-evaluate. You are important and deserve attention to your needs as well. It's time to give YOU the attention you need to set your world back into its proper balance.

Love Lynn

Your Health and Wellness

This section briefly discusses ideas regarding health and wellness. This advice should not replace the advice of a health professional. Consult your doctor before starting any new health regimen, exercise routine or diet.

We can have all of the best intentions and positive thoughts that we want, but if our physical bodies don't want to cooperate it is going to be difficult to achieve our goals on a day to day basis. We need plenty of energy if we want to THRIVE.

This is why it's crucial that you prioritize both your mental and physical health if you want to thrive in the area of self-love.

The food that we eat is equivalent to medicine. It's no coincidence that the nutrients that our bodies need to survive and thrive are present in fruits, vegetables and meats.

Yet many of us still treat food as if it's just here for pleasure. Many of us gorge on unhealthy, unnatural snacks and sugary drinks. We also feed it to our children. The health epidemic in the United States and beyond is mostly due to our poor eating habits, including fast food, sugar and fat (lard).

For instance, the health experts suggest that an average sized person eat no more than about 40 grams of added sugar per day (sugar that's added to food and drinks). Just one can of soda, which is not necessary for nutrition, has about 40 grams of sugar. A bottle of soda has more like 60 grams. Some of us drink several cans or bottles of soda every day, so what is that doing to our bodies?

Drink more water!

If you love yourself and your body, you have to take serious steps toward improving your diet and prioritizing physical fitness. Add more fruits, vegetables, fiber and protein to your diet as well as plenty of water to your daily intake and watch as you start to feel (and look) so much better. Eat more alkaline foods to keep your system in the proper balance—when your body is highly acidic instead of alkaline it is more prone to problems. There are charts available online that show you exactly which foods are alkaline (broccoli, kale, lemon juice, etc.) and which ones are acidic (beef, yeast, alcoholic beverages, fried foods, etc.).

Affirmations of good health (both physical and mental) are also important. Examine yourself from head to toe as you're getting dressed in the morning and say that you're healthy and whole with excitement and complete confidence. "I am the picture of good health and wellness!" You become what you think and talk about every day, so if you say you're healthy, and believe that you're healthy, then you're healthy. Believe it and live it.

There's one last thing I'd like to mention on the topic of health. I believe in the idea that disease can't thrive in a positive atmosphere. If you're living your life with a positive mental attitude, taking care of yourself, eating your nutrients, loving yourself and treating yourself like a queen (or king) your body responds by giving you good health in return.

Remember: The Only Opinion that Really Matters is Yours

The less you care about what other people think about you, the more powerful you become.

-- Love Lynn

After many years of allowing the opinions of others to rule my life, I have finally learned to stop caring so much about what other people think. People will try to break you down about everything from the clothes that you choose to wear, to the car that you drive, to how you wear your hair, to the way you choose to live your life in general.

One time when I was in college I went out with a guy who jokingly pointed out that I had a little mustache. My facial expression changed to pure disgust and needless to say I never saw him again. Now, since some guys personal opinion of how I look matters very little, I would have just laughed at it and cracked a joke back.

Everything is more fun and satisfying when you aren't worried about what someone else thinks. Even eating is more enjoyable because you can savor every bite in your own way without obsessing over having mustard on your face. If someone has a problem with the way you're enjoying your food, they can look away!

And of course, just about every woman can relate to the experiencing of having another woman look you up and down from head to toe. You can almost read the thoughts of judgment on her forehead. That used to bother me and make me self-conscious, but now it just makes me laugh.

One of the mantras that I live by is "only God can judge me." Other than my own opinion, His opinion is the only one that really matters to me when it comes right down to it. If I make a decision for my life and believe that God would approve, no one else can step in and tell me not to do it.

It becomes very easy to love yourself and believe in your own hype when you genuinely stop caring what other people think about the choices that you make for yourself. There's a saying:

What you think of me is none of my business!

If someone doesn't like you, that's their problem, not yours. As long as YOU genuinely like you, you're cool. This concept applies not just to you as a person, but to your work and creations.

You will never be able to please everyone. In fact, I don't think you should work hard to please anyone except yourself and God. If you spend your life trying to please other people you're not going to have much time left over to THRIVE.

Bringing It All Together—It All Comes Back to YOU

Have you ever gotten a great piece of information or learned something new, and the first thing that you want to do is tell someone else so that it can help *them*?

But what about you? Did you get all that you needed from that information first before trying to help someone else with it?

Some of us have a tendency to want to change the world and everyone around us, but don't put enough focus on improving our own lives. I can relate personally to that statement.

One of the most important lessons I learned while transforming my life for the better was that everything in my life comes down to me. I attract things to me. I decide how my life is going to be.

And my life today is a result of MY past actions, thoughts, behaviors and decisions. No one else is to blame (or able to take credit) for where I am in life.

Taking Full Personal Responsibility for YOUR Life

I am the master of my fate:

I am the captain of my soul.

-- From *Invictus* by William Ernest Henley

One of the hardest but most rewarding lessons that I had to learn during my journey was that I had to take full personal responsibility for what was happening in my life. In fact, this was the very first lesson I had to learn in order to make a real breakthrough.

Now that I'm aware of the blame that I was placing on the outer world for my inner turmoil, I see it happening all around me in other people. I see how quickly and naturally others will rush to point the finger at anyone they can, rather than stop and take full responsibility for what they have done to cause the situation. Some people find it almost impossible to take the blame for what happens in their lives. Here are a few examples:

- A woman gets fired from her job. She blames her boss for being a bitch or her co-workers for trying to take her down instead of taking accountability for being late almost every day, having a bad attitude and using Facebook/chatting all day long (this used to be me years ago).

- A man is dumped by his girlfriend or wife. He blames her for being disloyal and a "whore" instead of admitting that he neglected her and treated her disrespectfully for years. OR that he simply chose the wrong woman to be with.

- A pet eats your dinner. You blame the pet for being hungry and doing what animals do instead of blaming yourself for leaving the plate exposed on your table.

The right thing to do in these situations is to take responsibility for the role you played in what went wrong. And you know, as much as we hate to do it at first, something funny and strange happens when you openly and fully take responsibility for your role. Some people will go out of their way to help you through it!

You see, your boss is expecting you to argue with him about why you were chatting on the internet all day or smoking in the bathroom or late for work. That's what most people do, and that's why most people end up getting fired or having a stressful relationship with their employer. But what your boss doesn't expect is that you will say

"I apologize, I was completely wrong here. I don't know what came over me. Will you forgive me?"

You assume that this type of response will make you look stupid and weak, but au contraire! It's actually powerful. When you accept responsibility for your fault in the situation, you may be surprised at how the other person rushes to your defense and may even tell you to just forget about it altogether. This concept is discussed in more detail in the book *The 7 Habits of Highly Effective People* by Stephen R. Covey. If you're having problems dealing with people, even the most difficult types, you've got to read this book.

While out driving one time, it was pouring down rain outside. A light turned from yellow to red and I cruised right on through it. I didn't want to screech to a stop in the rain. I looked to the left and saw an officer sitting right there watching me. I sighed and pulled my car over before the officer even had a chance to put on her lights.

When she came to my window, I didn't try to come up with an excuse or get upset at having to stop—I just handed her my information and explained, "I didn't want to brake abruptly in the rain, but I apologize because I was in the wrong."

She left for just a few minutes, came back and told me to go ahead and enjoy my day.

Now if I had sucked my teeth and snapped at the officer for interrupting my day over something so minor, as many people choose to do, what would have probably happened?

Instead of going for that kneejerk reaction of blaming any and everybody else but yourself for why you didn't do what you were supposed to do, take full responsibility for it instead. In my experience, people will respect you more and things will fall right into place.

Here's a blog post that I wrote about taking responsibility:

Blog Post—12/22/13—FWB Sucks

I Did It; It's My Fault: Taking Personal Responsibility for Your Life

"Bite the dog that bit you."

"Ooooo, she makes me so mad!"

"The devil made me do it."

These are all common phrases that people use to absolve themselves of personal responsibility. When something doesn't go right, the first thing we tend to do is look for someone or something to blame.

At some point in your life, you have to stand up and say: "It was me, I did it. I did it to myself."

There aren't many things that you can honestly blame on others. For instance, say a child went astray and turned to drugs as a teen. It's not his friend's fault or the girl he's decided to with, it's the fault of his parents for not instilling more integrity and morals in him as a child. Once that child becomes an adult, it's his own fault why he keeps getting into trouble.

If you find yourself in a string of abusive relationships or constantly being used up by men, you can't blame that on anyone else but your own choices. There's a pattern there, which begins and ends with you.

"Bite the dog that bit you"—YOU bit yourself, time and time again by continuing to pick up that bottle and drink

"She makes me so mad!"—YOU are allowing someone else's negative energy to upset your life

"The devil made me do it."—no, YOU did the deed and if anything the devil probably just watched, laughing at your poor choices

The longer you continue to blame the outer world for your inner turmoil and the trouble in your life, the longer your problems will persist.

I Did It -- It Was Me

When you start to take full responsibility for what's going on in your life you'll be surprised at how FREE you will feel. You'll finally realize that you are the sole master of your destiny. All you have to do is change something that you're doing, saying, thinking or feeling and the problems will vanish. Even when you are faced with new obstacles, you'll be able to jump over them with the ease of a world-class hurdler.

Take stock of what's going on in your life today. What is holding you back from true happiness? Identify each and every "problem" you have going on in your life and take full responsibility for each of them.

Once you have done that, now you can get started on the SOLUTION.

Love Lynn

Follow Your Own Voice

I was once at a bar and saw an older woman falling down drunk. The woman was agitated and fighting everyone who tried to help her out, including me. The person I was with told me to just leave it alone and said we should leave.

I thought about it but then refused. I told him to go ahead home if he wanted. I continued to watch the woman. My companion decided to stay.

Finally the woman stumbled out of the bar into the street and I followed to make sure she got into a cab. She screamed at everyone to leave her alone and that she didn't want to live anymore. I saw her pain. Not long after that she fell in a heap on the street and couldn't move—exactly, what I had feared. As I called for help, I was astounded by the number of people who just kept walking by this woman in distress on the street.

There are times when you simply MUST go against the grain of what everybody else would do. You have to follow your own intuition, not what other people say. Don't be afraid to go against what other people say or do when you feel that it's necessary. If you want to live an exceptional life and THRIVE you absolutely must follow your own intuition.

Despite Popular Belief, You Can't Always Have It Your Way

Remember the story of the grasshopper and the ant? The grasshopper sings "oh, the world owes me a living." I heard that story countless times when I was young, but somehow the premise of that story escaped me until later on.

I used to blame everyone for everything that went wrong in my life. I blamed men for not treating me like a princess instead of taking responsibility for making the wrong choices in partners. I blamed my school for why I didn't get the jobs that I wanted when I graduated, when the truth was that I partied three days a week and that's why I didn't graduate at the top of my class.

In our modern culture, the American culture in particular, we are taught that we are supposed to have everything our way. We're taught about this American dream and the happiness that we're entitled to, but we forget the part that says we're only entitled to the *pursuit* of happiness.

I'm not sure where we get this idea that we deserve everything in life even when we're not willing to work for it, but it's that mentality that holds a lot of people back from achieving great things in life.

Learn to Let Go and Relax

There's one thing that I have learned over the years that some people may find difficult to grasp. It somewhat goes against what we've been taught about the necessity of working hard.

I have found that when something is *too* hard, it just might not be meant to be.

Let me clarify this statement. I don't think that you should give up on completing a task just because it's challenging. Challenging is one thing; continually problematic is another.

Once you set your sights on a task, things should move along smoothly.

When you are faced with snag after snag, problem after problem, issue after issue while trying to do something, there's a good chance it's a sign that this might not be the right way to go about things.

In my experience, when it's all smooth sailing, and you're just knocking down pin after pin as you go along, that's when you know you're on the right track.

Here's an example. On my blog I told the story of how I drove around looking for a Nutribullet to give someone as a gift when the store where I ordered it for "immediate pickup" suddenly changed the timeline from "immediate" to five weeks. I went from store to store where I lived looking for the Nutribullet but no one had it. Ironically, the only store that had it was the same one that I had purchased it from before, so I would have had to go to the same store that jerked me around, buy the item a second time, then wait for my money to be refunded on the first order.

As I was headed to the store, something told me to just go home and not worry about it. I did. I relaxed and enjoyed my evening.

As I was driving to my friend's house the next day, I passed right by a department store that I hadn't thought to check. They had the item, in stock, at the same price as the other one and all was well.

You've heard the saying "let go and let God." Well that's all this is about. Sometimes you have to let go of something that you're clutching way too tightly and stay tuned for new instructions. Release it and relax. Maybe there's a better way or a better solution available.

Can You Look at the Bright Side of Every Situation?

If you can get to a point in your life where you can see the bright side of even a challenging and tough situation, you are in a really good place. In fact, I think this is a quality that can help you conquer just about anything that comes your way as you navigate your life.

Try to see the blessing in even the smallest issues you run into. No food in the house until you do some grocery shopping that next day? Yay, pizza time! Missed a train? Maybe it's so that you can run right into an old friend at the station or have another cool experience. Released from a job? Okay, you'll look for another, and now you have more time to focus on your residual income plan.

I believe that the Universe is working in my favor and in yours. I believe that God wants us all to succeed and THRIVE. I believe that with each experience God is bringing us closer and closer to happiness and our purpose of bettering this world. So in each situation that I experience, I eventually stop and ask myself: "What is God trying to tell me or teach me here?"

Share Your Light

Spreading light and positivity is like using your candle to light other candles. Sharing your light doesn't diminish your own light—in fact it just makes the world around you brighter. Sharing your light also improves the chance that someone else will be able to light you back up when you need it the most. So share a smile, share a laugh, and lift someone up with a positive word or compliment. They need it as much as you do.

Keep these simple lessons in mind as you go through each day, and you will find yourself slowly sliding up that scale from barely surviving to THRIVING in your life.

I wish you **Happiness Light Love Peace and for Everything Good** to come your way from this moment forward!

Love Lynn

Visit my website for more insights at:
http://www.LifeLoveLynn.com

If you're having dating drama, visit:
http://www.LetHimChaseYou.com

For general self-esteem advice specifically related to dating and relationships visit:
http://www.FriendsWithBenefitsSucks.com

Email loveletter@lethimchaseyou.com to receive a link to a free copy of my special Love Letter (from You to You).

If you enjoyed this book or have used it to make a positive change in your life, I'd love to hear your story. Please submit your review to Amazon and/or send it to ***lynngeee9@gmail.com*** *. It may be published on my website or blog. Thank you!*

Love Lynn

- - -